it's a gas!

KINGFISHER
LONDON & NEW YORK

This selection copyright © Kingfisher 2011
Illustrations copyright © Martin Chatterton and Jane Eccles 2011
Published in the United States by Kingfisher,
175 Fifth Ave., New York, NY 10010
Kingfisher is an imprint of Macmillan Children's Books, London.

Distributed in the U.S. and Canada by Macmillan,
175 Fifth Ave., New York, NY 10010

Library of Congress Cataloging-in-Publication data has been applied for.

ISBN: 978-0-7534-6677-3

Kingfisher books are available for special promotions and premiums.
For details contact: Special Markets Department, Macmillan,
175 Fifth Ave., New York, NY 10010.

For more information, please visit www.kingfisherbooks.com

Typeset by Nigel Hazle

Printed and bound in the U.K. by CPI Mackays, Chatham ME5 8TD
1 3 5 7 9 8 6 4 2
0611

it's a Gas!

Illustrated by
Martin Chatterton and Jane Eccles

KINGFISHER
NEW YORK

Why was the stable boy so busy?

Because his work kept piling up!

What happened to the boy
who drank eight cans of cola?

He brought 7 UP.

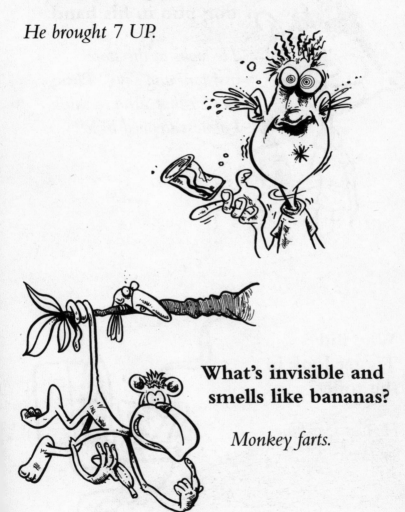

What's invisible and
smells like bananas?

Monkey farts.

A boy walks into a store with a big pile of dog poo in his hand.

He looks at the store assistant and says, "Phew, look at that. And to think I almost stepped in it!"

Why did Tigger look in the toilet?

He was searching for Pooh.

What do you call a fly with no eyes, no legs, and no wings?

A booger.

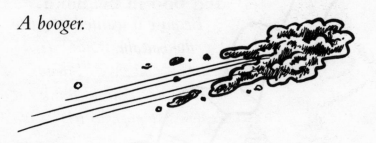

Man: I'd like some toilet paper, please.

Woman: What color would you like?

Man: Just give me white— I'll color it myself!

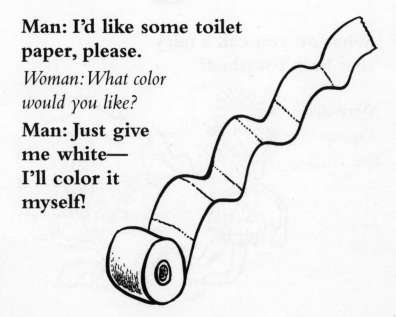

Why did the toilet paper roll down the hill?

Because it wanted to get to the bottom.

What do you call a fairy that hasn't washed?

Stinkerbell.

6

What do you get if you walk under a cow?

A pat on the head.

Why does Batman wear his underwear outside his trousers?

To keep them clean.

Knock, Knock!
Who's there?
Donna.
Donna who?
**Donna sit there—
someone peed on
the seat!**

What goes ho ho, plop plop?

Santa Claus on the toilet.

Tom had to go to the doctor because every time he tried to speak he farted.

"You must *(fffaaaart)* help me, Doctor, it's so *(whwhhiffleeee)* embarrassing. The only good thing *(pfflllpfflll)* is that my farts *(sssphhhwhee)* don't smell."

"Hmmm," said the doctor. "I will have to send you to a specialist."

"Will that be *(fffaaaart)* a bottom specialist or a *(pfflllpflll)* surgeon?" asked Tom.

"Neither," said the doctor. "I'm sending you to a nose specialist. There's something very wrong with yours!"

**What do you get
if you cross a
skunk with
a dog?**

Rid of the dog.

**What do
dogs call parking meters?**

Pay toilets!

What's big and gray and has odor problems?

A smellyphant.

What's brown and sounds like a bell?

Dung.

Little Johnny is approached by the lifeguard at the public swimming pool.

"You're not allowed to pee in the pool," said the lifeguard. "I'm going to report you."

"But everyone pees in the pool," said Little Johnny.

"Maybe," said the lifeguard, "but not from the diving board."

What did Data see in the toilet?

The captain's log.

What do you call a dirty Teletubby?

Stinky-winky.

What do cannibals do at a wedding?

Toast the bride and groom.

What nut sounds like a sneeze?

A cashew.

Why do giraffes enjoy having such long necks?

Because their feet smell awful.

"**What's the difference between dog poo and chocolate?**"

"*I don't know.*"

"**In that case, remind me not to buy you any chocolate.**"

What kind of peas are brown?

Poopeas.

What's green and smelly?

The Incredible Hulk's farts.

What's the sharpest thing in the world?

A fart. It goes through your pants and doesn't even leave a hole.

What's huge, green, and sits around complaining all day?

The Incredible Sulk.

Why did Frankenstein's monster get indigestion?

He bolted down his food.

Which monster makes strange noises in its throat?

A gargoyle.

What goes ha, ha, ha, crash?

An alien laughing his head off.

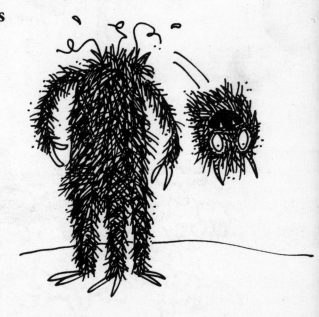

A belch is just one gust of wind
That cometh from the heart.
But should it take the
Downward route,
It turns into a fart.

What's wet, brown, and smells like peanuts?

Elephant puke.

What do you get if you cross an elephant with a parakeet?

A bird with a very dirty cage.

Why was the computer nut away from school?

He'd caught a computer bug.

First man: My dog has no nose.

Second man: How does he smell?

First man: Awful.

**What vegetable
can you find in
a toilet?**

A leek.

What's a dirty book?

One that's been dropped in the toilet.

What smells, runs all day, and lies around at night with its tongue hanging out?

A pair of old sneakers.

What's the difference between school lunches and horse poo?

School lunches are usually cold.

There was a young lady from Philly
Who cooked a large pot of chili.
She ate the whole lot
Straight from the pot
And ran to the john in a jiffy!

Stacy: I've just bought a pig.

Tracy: Where are you going to keep it?

Stacy: In the kitchen.

Tracy: But what about all the smell and mess?

Stacy: The pig will just have to get used to it!

**What do you get
if you cross a
skunk with
an owl?**

*Something
that smells
but doesn't
give a hoot!*

**How many skunks does it take to raise
a big stink?**

A phew.

What do you get if you eat baked beans and onions?

Tear gas.

What did the skunk say when the wind changed direction?

"It's all coming back to me now."

Three very thirsty men were trekking through the desert and came across a magician. The magician was standing at the top of a slide. The magician said, "You may each go down the slide, asking for a drink. When you reach the bottom, you will land in a huge refreshing pool of the drink you have asked for."

The first man went down and yelled, "Lemonaaaaade!"

The second man went down and yelled, "Cooooke!"

The third man went down and yelled, "Wheee-eeeeee!"

Why did the boy bring toilet paper to the birthday party?

Because he's a party pooper.

What's green and smells?

An alien's nose.

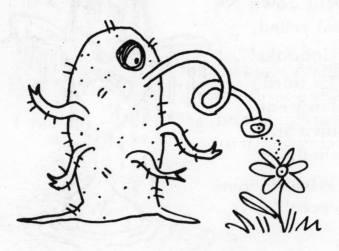

What's the difference between a huge, ugly, smelly monster and a piece of candy?

People like candies.

What's worse than taking a bite of your apple and seeing a worm?

Seeing half a worm.

Birdie, Birdie in the sky
Dropped some white stuff in my eye.
I'm a big girl, I won't cry—
I'm just glad that cows don't fly.

Did you hear the joke about the fart?

You don't want to—it stinks!

What does the Queen do if she breaks wind?

She issues a royal pardon.

How many rotten eggs were in the omelette?

A phew!

How can you help a starving cannibal?

Give him a hand.

Knock, Knock!

Who's there?

Butter.

Butter who?

Butter be quick—I need the toilet!

Why wouldn't the skeleton go bungee jumping?

Because he didn't have the guts.

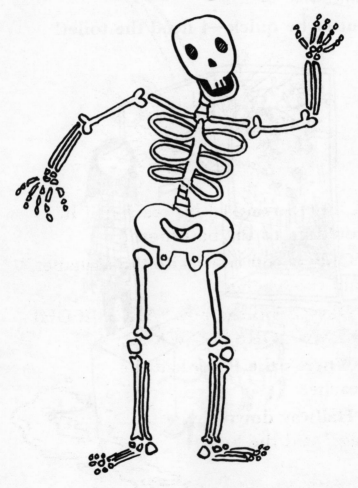

If you sprinkle when you tinkle,
Please be sweet and wipe
the seat.

A little boy asked his teacher if he
could go to the bathroom.

"Only if you can recite the alphabet,"
said the teacher.

"Okay," said the boy. "ABCDEFGHI
JKLMNOQRSTUVWXYZ."

"Where's the P?" asked the
teacher.

"Halfway down my
leg," said the boy.

**How can you stop a
skunk from smelling?**

Put a peg on its nose.

**Pardon me, it was not me—
It was my food.
It just popped up to say hello,
And now it's gone back down below.**

What's the last thing to go through a fly's mind before he hits the windshield?

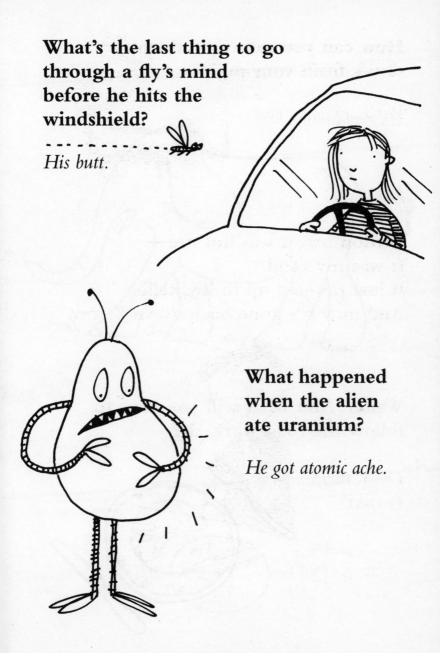

His butt.

What happened when the alien ate uranium?

He got atomic ache.

How can you tell when there's an elephant in your pudding?

It's very lumpy.

Waiter: And what will you have to follow the roast pork, sir?

Diner: Indigestion, I expect.

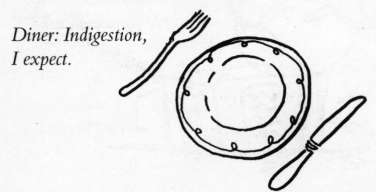

Did you hear the one about the constipated mathematician?

He worked it out with a pencil!

Melissa: Do you know anyone who has been on the TV?

Jason: My brother did once, but he uses the toilet now.

Charlie: What do you clean your top teeth with?

Bob: A toothbrush and toothpaste.

Charlie: And your bottom?

Bob: The same.

Charlie: Oh gross, I use toilet paper.

Why did the alien take a bath?

So he could make a clean getaway.

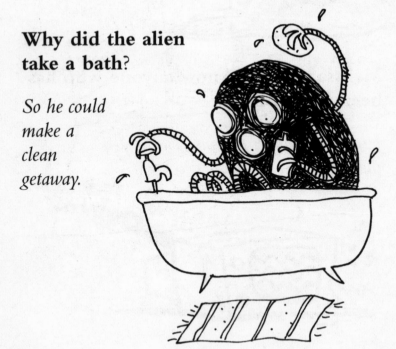

How can you tell when a gorilla's been in the refrigerator?

By the hairs in the butter.

Why can't you hear a pterodactyl go to the bathroom?

Because it has a silent "p".

Why do doctors and nurses wear masks?

So if they make a mistake, the patient won't know who did it.

An elderly woman is riding in an elevator in a very luxurious hotel when a young, beautiful woman gets in, smelling of expensive perfume. She turns to the old woman and says snootily, "It's called *Romance*, and it costs $50 a bottle." Then another young, beautiful woman smelling of perfume gets in and says, also very snootily, "*Eternal*, $100 a bottle." About three floors later the elderly woman has reached her destination and is about to leave the elevator. She turns around, looks right into the eyes of both of the young women, farts loudly, and says, "Broccoli— 49 cents a pound!"

**How does a
cannibal greet
a guest?**

"Pleased to eat you."

**Why is it foolish
to upset a
cannibal?**

*You might find
yourself in hot water.*

**What do you get
if you cross a
fish with a pig?**

Wet and dirty.

**What's special about a birthday cake
made with baked beans?**

*It's the only cake that can blow its own
candles out.*

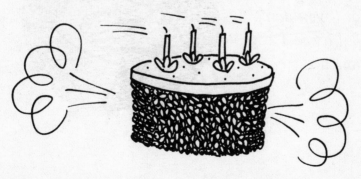

I sat next to a duchess
at tea.
It was just as I
feared it would be.
Her rumbling
abdominal
Was simply
phenomenal,
And everyone
thought it was me.

I'm going to have
to let one rip—do
you mind?

*Not if you don't
mind when I
throw up.*

What's brown, smelly, and sits on a piano stool?

Beethoven's last movement.

What do you do if you give an elephant chili?

Get out of the way.

Has the bottom fallen out of your world?

Eat prunes, and then the world will fall out of your bottom.

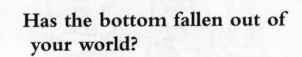

Knock, Knock!
Who's there?
Ivan.
Ivan who?
Ivan itchy bottom.

What's the difference between a toilet brush and a cookie?

You can't dip a toilet brush in your hot chocolate!

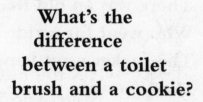

Teacher: Your son is very full of himself, isn't he?

Mother: Well, only when he's been biting his nails and picking his nose.

**There was an old man from Oket,
Who went for a ride in a rocket.
The rocket went bang,
His ears went twang,
And he found his nose in his pocket!**

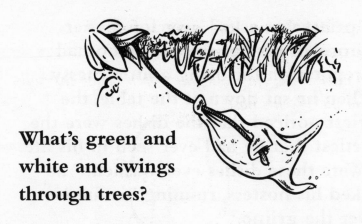

What's green and white and swings through trees?

Tarzan's hankie!

As Terry was getting ready to go to school, a button fell off of his shirt. When he opened his bedroom door, the handle fell off.

Now he's afraid to blow his nose!

A priest was asked over for dinner by one of his parishioners who had a reputation for being a little messy. When he sat down at the table, the priest noticed that the dishes were the dirtiest that he had ever seen in his life. "Were these dishes ever washed?" he asked his hostess, running his fingers over the grime.

She replied, "They're as clean as soap and water could get them."

The priest felt a little apprehensive but blessed the food anyway and started eating. It was really delicious, despite the dirty dishes, and he said so.

When dinner was over, the hostess took the dirty dishes outside and yelled to her dogs, "Here, Soap! Here, Water!"

"Mommy, why can't we have a garbage can like other people?"
"Shut up and keep eating!"

What do you get if you cross a skunk with a dinosaur?

A stinkasaurus.

How long is a minute?

*Depends how desperately
you have to go.*

If H$_2$O is on the inside of a fire hydrant, what is on the outside?

K$_9$P.

Notice in café: *All the drinking water in this café has been passed by the manager.*
Notice in bathroom: *In the interest of economy please use both sides of the toilet paper.*
Notice in butcher's: *Will customers please refrain from sitting on the bacon slicer as we are getting a little behind with our orders!*

"Doctor, doctor, I think I've been bitten by a vampire."
"Here, drink this glass of water."
"Will that make me feel better?"
"No, but we'll be able to see if your neck leaks!"

Taylor: My friend is built upside down . . .
Terry: What do you mean?
Taylor: His nose runs, and his feet smell!

What's the difference between a Brussels sprout and a booger?

You can't get a kid to eat Brussels sprouts.

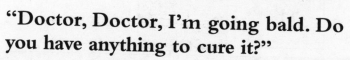

"Doctor, Doctor, I'm going bald. Do you have anything to cure it?"

"Yes, put one pound of horse poo on your head every morning."

"And will that cure me?"

"No, but no one will come close enough to see that you don't have any hair!"

Other titles in the **Sidesplitters** series you might enjoy: